Small

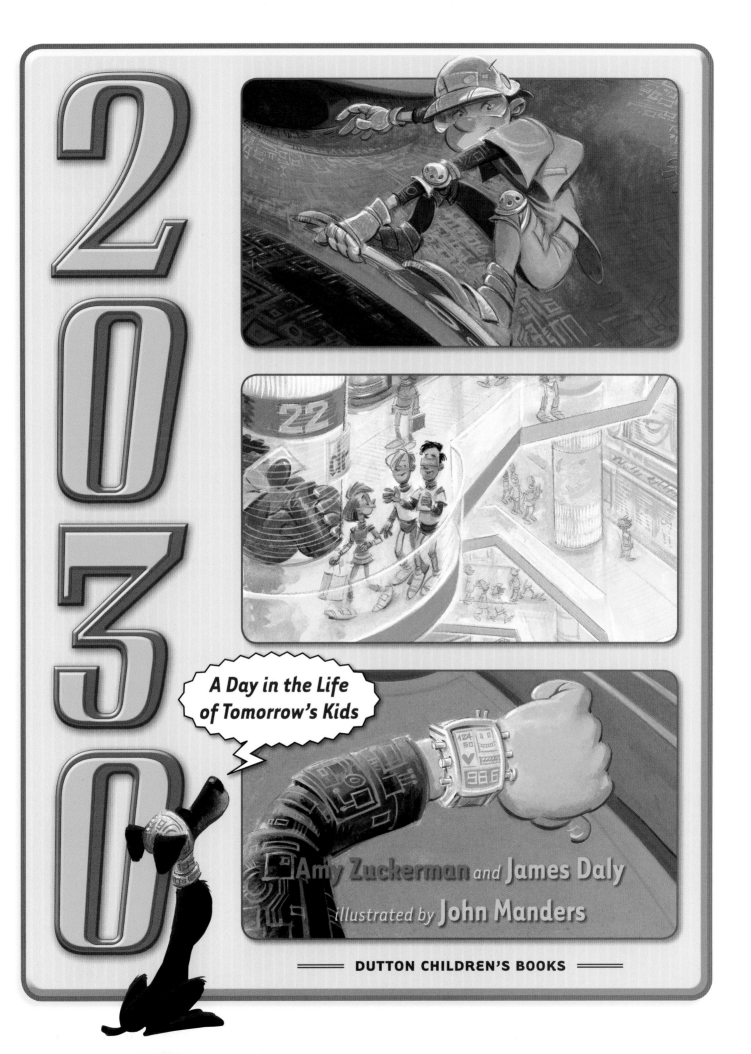

THINGS

It happens every day. You turn on the TV and before long there will be a commercial for something "new and improved." Car styles change. Clothing styles change. All because people—and their tastes—change.

If you ask your parents what life was like when they were kids, you might be surprised to hear that they didn't have many of the things you enjoy today. No cell phones, computers, or DVDs. Some never had VCRs. Ask your grandparents about their childhoods and you'll learn that some didn't even have TV. They listened to programs on the radio, and their imaginations provided the pictures.

COOL!

CHANGE.—

Every day, scientists, engineers, and other people with big imaginations come up with new ideas that change our lives. Before you know it, one of their inventions might appear in your home or school.

What will a kid's life be like many years from now? What sort of inventions will change kids' daily lives?

No one can predict exactly what is going to happen next, but by looking at our world today and asking some very smart scientists, engineers, and "futurists," we came up with a credible idea of what life might be like in the future.

So, buckle your seat belt and get ready—it's time to take a trip to the year 2030.

Time to get dressed. Your clothes may not look much different from the clothes of today, but they do things that today's jeans and jackets can't do. Tiny solar discs woven right into the material store sunlight and turn it into electricity—enough to run all of your portable electronic gadgets and games.

Morning light splashes into your bedroom as you wake up. You yawn and stretch, then notice an orange glow coming from the glass ball that sits on your night table. Someone is trying to reach you on the data orb.

Ooompf! Your dog, Willie, jumps on you, barks once, and then says—in perfect English—that he wants to go for a walk. Willie isn't really talking. What you hear is a voice synthesizer attached to his collar. This little computer translates his barks and body movements into simple words and phrases that tell you when he is hungry, playful, or just wants some company.

TIME FOR
A WALK!

Turning off Willie's speaker so you don't have to listen to him, you reach back to your data orb. An image starts taking shape. It's your friend's face looking at you (remember the witch's crystal ball in *The Wizard of Oz?*). "Don't forget to meet me at the skateboard park this afternoon," he says.

The data orb is one of the ways you stay in touch with people in the year 2030. It transmits and receives three-dimensional images from all over the world, so you can see what your friend is doing, what's going on in the neighborhood, or even what's happening at school.

Yes, there's still school in 2030.

Making breakfast is easy in 2030, because smart appliances, things like toasters and microwaves, can sense the world around them through sounds, voice, and body heat. These devices use a special computer language and wireless signals to send messages back and forth. You want your toast golden brown and eggs over easy? No problem. Everything's ready when you come down to breakfast.

Beep, beep! Beep, beep!

That's Clean-a-rella, your housecleaning robot. It can move around the house and do simple tasks like vacuuming and dusting. Housecleaning robots use artificial intelligence—computer programs that give them the ability to make decisions, just like people. Tiny sensors embedded in Clean-a-rella's cover transmit infrared light beams that bounce off objects in the robot's path to keep it from bumping into furniture or running over toys.

Dad's already downstairs in his office. Like many workers in 2030, he runs a home-based business using the Internet, which allows people to live and work in the same place. Working out of homes saves companies the cost of maintaining big buildings that use electricity, heat, and air-conditioning. It also cuts down on pollution, because people don't have to drive their cars to work.

The world outside does not look very different. There are houses and trees, and the sky is still blue. But somehow, it isn't the same. For one thing, there are more kids.

In 2030, there are over six million more elementary-school kids in the United States—that means for every five kids there are today, there is an extra one. Time to get a bigger school bus! There are many more adults, too. In the United States alone there are over a half billion people; many of them are senior citizens. The odds of you celebrating someone's one-hundredth birthday are three times greater than they were thirty years ago.

Because the population is aging, there is a need for more health-care professionals. Mom's a physical therapist who works with older people at a retirement center a few blocks away. She helps them perform exercises so they can move easier and feel better.

Most people live in suburbs outside the cities in areas called cluster developments. These are houses and apartments that are connected to a common yard or playground. The development in which you live is also an eco-village.

Everything in your eco-village—from the materials used to build houses to the way the lawn is maintained—is good for the earth. The water you use to wash your hands is filtered and then recycled to grow plants. The sun's rays are collected through solar discs that are built into roofs and then converted into electricity to light and cool homes. Large turbines turn wind energy into electricity, and even garbage is reused to help grow flowers and vegetables.

Before long, you arrive at school. The building looks normal. But the way it's made is different. The materials used aren't wood, steel, or even plain concrete. They're special plasticized concrete blocks with built-in wiring and plumbing. They snap together just like toy bricks. You can even move the walls around to change the shape of a room.

On the surface of the building and windows is a thin coating of cells that collects energy to help control the building's temperature. Just like the fibers in your clothing, the building surface becomes dark when it's cloudy and light when it's sunny.

You learn that there are almost 800 million people living in or around the cities of Africa. That's almost the same number of people living in all of Africa at the beginning of the twenty-first century. Because so many people moved to the cities looking for jobs, there is not enough food or shelter to support the population. Many of them are young, because a terrible disease called AIDS killed so many adults in Central Africa during the early part of the century. Tomorrow you'll bring in some dried food for the class collection for the United Nations' African relief operation.

In social studies class your teacher asks you to find an article on your computer about Central Africa. By 2030, the Web has become so enormous that you need a tool called a personal agent to help you. This humanlike, three-dimensional figure asks you all sorts of questions and then gets you just what you need, sort of like your very own butler.

Your teacher announces that it's time for a "trip" to ancient Egypt, in northern Africa. The room darkens and screens drop down from the ceiling. Suddenly, pyramids appear from all sides. It seems like you can walk up and touch them. These are giant holograms—

special photographs made with the aid of a laser. When a hologram is lit in just the right way, a three-dimensional image appears.

By 2030, individual holographic images can be projected so rapidly that they appear to move. That's why you and your classmates feel as though you're traveling through the Egyptian desert and not just watching a movie.

The class down the hall is in the Multimedia Production and Research Center. The students are learning how to use a high-resolution display screen that creates clear pictures from both the front and the back. On the screen you can combine pictures, words, and video just by talking into the computer.

The kids are creating special video presentations of their families. Many of them have relatives all over the world, because in 2030 it's common for people from different countries and ethnicities to marry. One girl goes online to China and asks her dad's sister to say a few words she can record. Then she reaches her mom's cousin in the Dominican Republic, who agrees to transmit some video clips and native music. When the teacher signals, she pushes the PRESENT button and the room is filled with pictures and sounds.

Some kids are practicing skiing moves over at the virtual ski area. You strap yourself into the ski machine, which moves up and down and from side to side to mimic the shape of a mountain. The machine will let you know when you're off balance without letting you fall. That last bump sure felt rough!

The bell rings for recess. You go straight to virtual batting practice in the gym and pick up a plastic bat and a virtual reality headset. When you put on the headset, you feel as though you've stepped right onto a baseball field. It's a clear day, and the other players are waiting for you.

Whoosh! The first pitch is a curve. You swing and miss.

Whoosh! again. This time it's high and fast. *CRACK!* You knock a single right up the middle.

Tired of batting practice? There's still time to join a bunch of kids on the smart trampoline. It looks like a regular trampoline, but there are hundreds of tiny electronic sensors woven into the material that instantly measure the weight, bounce, and strength of each jumper. The surface changes from loose to firm to give the best jumps possible. Everyone's bouncing at different heights and speeds. It's just like flying.

Briiiiing!

The bell rings and it's time for lunch.

In 2030, food can be altered so that your brain thinks that even the foods you hate to eat, like Brussels sprouts, taste delicious. That's because scientists have discovered the part of your brain that controls taste and flavors. So you'll be happy to eat healthy things.

On your tray is a tofu burger that tastes like a real hamburger. Your soy drink looks and tastes like the double-chocolate shake at the ice-cream shop, and your broccoli spears look and taste just like French fries!

Blooooop! Bleeeep! Blooooop!

That's your watch reminding you to beam your health information to the doctor's office for your appointment on Saturday. Push a button and the health gauge on your watch automatically sends information on blood pressure, body temperature, and even your feelings directly to your doctor's office.

Wouldn't it be great if you never had to visit the doctor? Sorry, but you can't get out of visiting in person. The doctor needs to upgrade your disease-fighting robots. These almost invisible mechanical robots with mini-computer "brains" are injected into your body to fight diseases. They look like specks of dust on your hand, but they are powerful. They fight nasty colds by slowly releasing medicine and vitamins.

At the end of the school day, Grandma picks you up in her automated car. You're off to the mall to shop for clothes. Most cars in 2030 are equipped with eco friendly fuels that reduce pollution and a satellite-controlled global positioning system that talks to smart roadways. Traffic signals sense your approaching car, and if there is no traffic coming from the other direction, they turn green automatically. The same technology can also control your car's movement and get you to your destination without you ever touching a steering wheel.

EMERGENCY USE ONLY!

Almost everything you buy can be ordered on the Web at home. But it's still fun to go to the mall, which is the size of a small town. There are moving tracks so you don't have to walk the long distances from shop to shop, and all sorts of streaming Web hologram advertisements line the walls—it's almost like visiting an amusement park.

At the Clothing Order Center, you provide your size and the clerk conducts a computer search of all the stores in the mall—over one thousand of them—to find what you want. But for that special outfit for your cousin's wedding, he suggests the customized clothing shop on Level 22.

At the shop, a clerk uses a hand-held scanner to direct infrared beams at you to determine your exact measurements in seconds. This information is fed into a computer that creates a three-dimensional image of your body. You can dress the computer model in any style of clothing you want. The fabric, color, and even buttons and zippers are your choice.

"We'll deliver it to you by Saturday," the salesperson says with a smile.

SLEEVE
LENGTH
14.5"

UNDER
PANTS:
GIRLS M

INSEAM:18
JACKET:2
WRIST:16

SHOES:
6 WIDE

CUSTOMER:
605BCM1

Home—finally. Grabbing some peanut-butter crackers, you take off to meet some buddies at the skateboard park. Once you're inside, a friend lets you try some kick flips on his smart magnetized skateboard. Amazing—it hovers over the ground just like a magic carpet! OK, maybe you're just a couple of feet off the ground, but you'll feel like you're flying. Think of the awesome moves you can do!

Hold two magnets apart, then bring one close to the other. One side is drawn toward the first magnet, but when you flip the magnet around, the other side is pushed away or repelled. That is how the smart skateboard works. Powerful magnets are placed under the floor to create a force field that actually pushes your board into the air. Lean forward and you're on your way. Lightweight stabilizers keep your board steady, and embedded sensors keep you from crashing into things.

After the park, it's back home, do your homework, and then eat. You can't wait to finish dinner so you can go to the eco-village's Fanta-trek Center. That's a special room outfitted with three-dimensional videos, plus touch and smell technologies so you feel like you have entered a fantasy world.

Tonight's program is "A Return to the Dinosaurs." Once you enter, you feel like you're in prehistoric times. You see the landscape and even smell the warm, humid earth of millions of years ago. To your right, baby dinosaurs are cracking out of their eggs, and over yonder are two raptors fighting it out by a stream.

It's late when you return home. You don't even complain when Mom and Dad tell you it's time for bed. It sure has been a busy day in 2030.

Your toothbrush contains toothpaste that squirts right into your mouth, which makes the whole brushing thing a little less messy. Yawning, you toss on some pajamas and slip under the covers.

Your data orb reminds you that it is almost time to go to sleep, so before you turn out the lights, you decide to reach for your favorite type of entertainment. It's light and easy to handle. The insides are soft and perfect for viewing, and it has provided kids and adults entertainment for many centuries.

You drift off to sleep. . .

. . . reading a book.

BIBLIOGRAPHY

BOOKS · JOURNALS · REPORTS

Ainsworth, Don. "Living the Sustainable Life," *Our Environment*, April 1997, Volume 2, Issue 3.

Alba, Richard D. "Assimilations Quiet Tide," *The Public Interest*, No. 119, Spring 1995. U.S. Census Bureau population projections posted on www.census.gov; Science Blog Website under IBOT.

Barry, Patrick. "Tiny Particles Target Big Diseases," *SciTini*, Boston University College of Communications, November 14, 2006. http://www.bu.edu/phpbin/news-cms/news/?dept=1127&id=41730&template=226.

Chen, Milton and Stephen D. Arnold. "A Day in the Life of a Young Learner," *2020 Visions*, U.S. Department of Commerce publication.

Earth Rights Institute. *"Ecovillage Development,"* June 20, 2008. http://www.earthrights.net/ecovillages.

"A Blend of Technology to Achieve Brilliant Colors and Designs," Fibre2fashion.com, May 22, 2008. http://www.fibre2fashion.com/news/textile-technology/newsdetails.aspx?news_id=56658.

Kaku, Michio. *Visions*. Anchor Books, 1998, pp. 31–66.

Nuemann, Ulrich and Chris Kyriaksis. "2020 Classroom," *2020 Visions*, U.S. Department of Commerce publication.

Pink, Daniel. *Free Agent Nation*. Warner Business Books, 2001.

Walczak, Diane. "Encompassing Education," *2020 Visions*, U.S. Department of Commerce publication.

Zimmerman, Delore. "An Appraisal of the Optimum City," *The Humboldt Journal of Social Relations*, Spring/Summer, 1982, Volume 9, Number 2.

Zuckerman, Amy. "Hidden Tech in the Valley: At the Cutting Edge of the Global Internet Economy." Western Massachusetts Electric Co., November 2002.

The UIUC Physics Van, part of the University of Illinois Physics Department in Champaign/Urbana, Illinois, and "Magnetic Levitation," an exploration project of the Lakeland Copper Beech Middle School in Yorktown Heights, New York.

NEWS SOURCES (INCLUDING WEB BASED)

"South Africa: Study Reveals the Grim Extent of HIV/AIDS," *Black World Today* Website, December 2, 2002.

Breitbart.com. "Robot-driven Cars to Hit Roads by 2030," February 17, 2008. http://www.breitbart.com/article.php?id=070218000644.7dauizys&show_article=1.

CBS News. "AIDS Cases on the Rise: By 2030 It Is Forecast to Be among Top 3 Causes of Death Worldwide," November 27, 2006.

Cherry, Dr. Reginald B., M.D. "Older Americans with Arthritis Expected to Double by 2030," *Christianpost.com*, June 18, 2008. http://www.christianpost.com/article/2008618/older-americans-with-arthritis-expected-to-double-by-2030.htm.

"The End of Petrolhead: Tomorrow's Cars May Just Plug In," *The Economist*, June 21-27, 2008.

"Microchips in the Blood," *The Economist Technology Quarterly*, September 21, 2002, p. 7.

"Relishing the Flavour," *The Economist Technology Quarterly*, June 22, 2002; Newsweek, E-paper, November 25, 2002, p. 68.

"Solar Cells Go Organic," *The Enomonist Technology Quarterly*, June 22, 2002, p. 6.

Health News Blog.com. "Wristwatch Helps with Supervision of Elderly Patients," August 4, 2006. http://www.healthnewsblog.com/seniors/

"Bake-off, 2049: The Winner!," *Newsweek*, June 2, 2000, p. 77.

"Spaces: Oh, the Places We'll Go!" *Newsweek*, January 1, 2000, pp. 66–67.

"Fabrics Smart Enough to Change Colors and Keep You Dry," *New York Times* Web archives, June 13, 2002.

Pentland, William. Forbes.com. "Big Oil's Hydrogen Future," June 20, 2008. http://www.forbes.com/home/2008/06/19/natural-gas-hydrogen-biz-energy-cx-wp 0620natgas.html.

Samuelson, Robert J. "The Spirit of America," *Newsweek*, January 13, 2003.

TMCnet.com. "Japanese Ventures Team up to Expand Home-use Robot Market," June 20, 2008. http://www.tmcnet.com/usubmit/2008/06/18/3504368.htm.

Tomsho, Robert. "Wind Shift in Energy Debate," *The Wall Street Journal*, June 19, 2008

With all my love to Julia, my daughter and muse, and to her long-ago friends at the Pelham (Mass.) Elementary School who have been my stalwart readers and "editors": Audrey Gould, Shayna Goss, Sarah Martini, Jovanna Robinson-Hidas, Savannah Stuitje, and Taylor Wilson.   —A.Z.

Thanks to my wife, Laura, for her endless love and support, and special hugs of appreciation to Samantha, Jackson, and Charlotte, my own glimpses of the future. Thanks also to Mom and Dad, who were always thinking about what's next.   —J.D.

To Aldous Huxley, these illustrations are humbly dedicated.   —J.M.

ACKNOWLEDGMENTS: The authors offer thanks to the following professionals who lent time, expertise, and inspiration to this project: Gregg Favalora, President, Actuality Systems, Burlington, MA; Rob Larsen, Program Manager, Draper Labs, Cambridge, MA; Paul Saffo of the Institute for the Future; Economist George Gilder; David Rose, Former President of Ambient Devices, Cambridge, MA; Kirk McElwain, Public Relations Director, Continental Automated Buildings Association; Charles Mann, a contributing correspondent to Science magazine and the Atlantic Monthly; Michael Walton, Cockrell Chair of Engineering, the LBJ School of Public Affairs at the University of Texas, Austin; Christopher Wilson, Director, Strategic Research at Tele Atlas, Palo Alto, CA; Ray Kurzweil, Head, Kurzweil Technologies; Ron Eccles, Head, Common Cold Centre, Cardiff, Wales; Joel Kotkin, author of The New Geography (Random House, 2000, 2001); Zenia Kotval, Ph.D., AICP, Assistant Professor, Michigan State University; J. Donald Moon, Professor of Government, Wesleyan University; Alan Hurwitz, principal of Alan Hurwitz Associates, an international consultant firm based in Amherst, MA; Rich Karlgaard, publisher of Forbes; John Kelly, scenario planner and researcher for A-Z International Associates, Berkeley, CA; Lance Winslow, Online Think Tank Coordinator; children's authors Jane Yolen and Corinne Demas, and Sarah Moon, poet and teacher.

The information provided by these experts serves as an addendum to our bibliography.

DUTTON CHILDREN'S BOOKS ★ A division of Penguin Young Readers Group

PUBLISHED BY THE PENGUIN GROUP

Penguin Group (USA) Inc., 375 Hudson Street, New York, New York 10014, U.S.A. ★ Penguin Group (Canada), 90 Eglinton Avenue East, Suite 700, Toronto, Ontario M4P 2Y3, Canada (a division of Pearson Penguin Canada Inc.) ★ Penguin Books Ltd, 80 Strand, London WC2R 0RL, England ★ Penguin Ireland, 25 St Stephen's Green, Dublin 2, Ireland (a division of Penguin Books Ltd) ★ Penguin Group (Australia), 250 Camberwell Road, Camberwell, Victoria 3124, Australia (a division of Pearson Australia Group Pty Ltd) ★ Penguin Books India Pvt Ltd, 11 Community Centre, Panchsheel Park, New Delhi—110 017, India ★ Penguin Group (NZ), 67 Apollo Drive, Rosedale, North Shore 0632, New Zealand (a division of Pearson New Zealand Ltd) ★ Penguin Books (South Africa) (Pty) Ltd, 24 Sturdee Avenue, Rosebank, Johannesburg 2196, South Africa ★ Penguin Books Ltd, Registered Offices: 80 Strand, London WC2R 0RL, England

Library of Congress Cataloging-in-Publication Data
Zuckerman, Amy.
2030 / by Amy Zuckerman and James Daly ; illustrated by John Manders.
p. cm.
ISBN: 978-0-525-47860-7
1. Technological forecasting—Juvenile literature. 2. Technological innovations—Forecasting—Juvenile literature. 3. Twenty-first century—Forecasts—Juvenile literature.
I. Daly, James. II. Manders, John, ill. III. Title.
T174.Z83 2009
601'.12—dc22   2008014606

Published in the United States by Dutton Children's Books,
a division of Penguin Young Readers Group
345 Hudson Street, New York, New York 10014
www.penguin.com/youngreaders

Designed by Jason Henry
Manufactured in China ★ First Edition
1 3 5 7 9 10 8 6 4 2